# Praise for Preserving Generational Wealth

"Working with MR. Douglas has been illuminating. He is keen on sharing his wealth of knowledge with everyone inclined to tap from it, and having a down-to-earth nature allows him to pass along complex financial lessons in the most digestible manner which I appreciate. This book is a pleasure to read because I know that he practices the wealth principles being shared here in his individual and family affairs. Watching him be a success is proof that they work. These principles are profitable to know and practice, especially starting at a younger age"

– **Kalu Kalu**
CEO
KICK&CO Synergy LTD.

"The cover of this book is striking and shows what Douglas is about—Family. I like the way examples of real scenarios are introduced all over the book to drive points home because this book appeals to people of all ages and is easy to understand. Kudos to you, Douglas for making the complex world of wealth preservation feel like a casual conversation over a cup of coffee. The book is a great blend of financial strategy and personal storytelling with the examples given. You've made it not only informative but also engaging. I found myself nodding in agreement on several occasions."

– **Emeka Offor**
Entrepreneur, Business Mogul
VCP Hotel, Lagos, Nigeria

"This book is a testament to Douglas's passion for empowering others. The sincerity with which he shares wealth strategies and systems is not only relatable but also inspiring. It's like getting a backstage pass to his journey, and I couldn't help but feel motivated to take charge of anywhere I may be a step behind in my financial journey."

– **Regina Eze**
Senior Clinical Research Associate
INC Research

# PRESERVING GENERATIONAL WEALTH

# PRESERVING GENERATIONAL WEALTH

Why The One Percent Never Start from Scratch
and How to Give Your Heirs the Same Edge

DOUGLAS A.C. EZE

Creating Generational Wealth®

Published by Largo Financial Services, LLC.



Largo Financial Services, LLC.
6401 Golden Triangle Dr #201, Greenbelt, MD 20770

Visit our website: https://buildwealthwithdouglas.com/

ISBN: 978-0-9899515-4-8

Curated and edited by: KICK&CO Synergy LTD. (www.kickandcosynergy.com)

# Dedication

This book is dedicated to my wonderful wife and my remarkable kids. I operate in this world to make it better as much as I can, and you all make me the best version of myself.

# CONTENTS

# FOREWORD

IN THE CAPTIVATING PAGES of Preserving Generational Wealth, Douglas A. C. Eze masterfully unveils the blueprint for generational wealth—revealing the art of not just acquiring riches but orchestrating a legacy of prosperity. With profound insights, he guides readers through the intricate steps of receiving, preserving, and passing down wealth.

Douglas A. C. Eze is a proven wealth architect, designing overall financial strategies that equip those he serves with the tools required to escape from economic bondage. He has dedicated his career to helping clients—ranging from everyday professionals and middle-American families to global leaders and public figures—understand, embrace, and employ strategies to create and sustain generational wealth. In a culture that makes flashy marketing and "get rich quick" promises easily accessible, Douglas's proof of performance separates him from the masses. He has invested extensive time and effort in mastering financial principles and products, developing powerful knowledge that allows him to exceed his clients' expectations.

This is not just a financial guide; it profoundly explores the foundations that empower future generations. If you aspire to elevate your heirs to the same stage where the one percent commence, Douglas's strategies are your indispensable tools. This book is not just a read; it is a transformative journey toward securing a lasting financial advantage for future generations.

– **LaFern Kitt Batie**
CEO
The Batie Group

# INTRODUCTION

WHEN I STUDIED WEALTHY FAMILIES that had succeeded in creating astounding amounts of wealth, I saw that they weren't just going to let all that effort and business fade to nothing. They were also working hard, maybe even twice as hard to ensure that they never lost their money. Warren Buffet's rule about how to stay wealthy—"never lose your money"—is perhaps something to live by if one is serious about preserving wealth. Just don't lose it!

But how do you keep from losing your money? The answer is that you deploy as much effort as you did in creating it, protecting it, and transferring it to worthy heirs who are equipped to steward it.

I accomplished what I set out to do with the first book, and I have succeeded in helping hundreds of businesses and families directly, and thousands indirectly.

The strategies and concepts made available in *Creating Generational Wealth*® showed readers how to get their finances in order and start building generational wealth. Many people reached out to me to express how glad they were to learn about the systems laid out in the book. After a couple of years, I started noting an increasing number of people who had succeeded in building generational wealth. It is more wealth than they can spend in their lifetime, thanks to the strategies laid out in my first book, but they all seemed to grow the same worry: "With this newfound wealth, how can we ensure our children get their hands on it smoothly, without any losses or hassles in transition?" That one question kept popping up. People were increasingly agitating for a new system for wealth: the next step, one that would ensure their heirs steward their wealth correctly and have a better starting point than they had.

After generational wealth is created, how is it transferred? Your business is up and running, but how do you go about operating like the super-successful families who keep wealth preserved across generations?

That is the question this book will answer. How do you protect your wealth from fizzling out, mismanagement, inflation, the government, or any other system that swallows wealth? How do you protect against unforeseen events and guarantee steady wealth growth regardless of times, trends, or market tailspins? I have worked with clients and their families to help them set up systems that address these concerns and more.

That knowledge is what has been made available in this book. This is the information that super successful business owners and families teach their kids and what you must start teaching yours to position them to play on a level playing field.

In the first book, we explored an anecdote that introduced David and Lisa—a family who grew their business, built multigenerational wealth, and made use of smart money vehicles like cash-value life insurance to park their wealth for the next generations. We met their son David Jr., who benefitted from his parents' smart business and money decisions and successfully inherited the money from them.

We also saw their grandson, Gerald, who didn't know about the life insurance policy his parents had taken out on him until they passed on. You see, David Jr. had learned a great deal from his parents and understood the value of planning ahead because he reaped the benefits firsthand. David Jr. graduated from college without debts and had taken out a life insurance policy on his son, Gerald, even without his knowledge. In this book, we will learn what heirs like David Jr. and Gerald do to protect the wealth stacked up for them by the generation before them, as well as how they steward that wealth, increase it, and successfully pass it on like good stewards to the next generation after them.

This is the knowledge that super successful business owners know that you need to know and share with your heirs. For many super successful businesspeople, the first generation must consider possibilities and occurrences years in advance, to plan properly and forestall unwanted events as well as set up a bright starting position for their heirs. You can do exactly what they did to ensure your generation doesn't struggle through many of the hurdles you did. Arguments can be made for why challenges shape character, but you will also agree that leaving a legacy of wealth and financial literacy for your generation also shapes their character in an equally desirable way. The world is modeled after the jungle idea that the bigger consumes the smaller. One blessing you can give to your kids is to let them have all the tools necessary to compete equally with any big entity in society. Knowledge is power. Even without all the money in the world, they can still operate at such a high level without being trampled upon by the rat race of society or the **one** percent earners.

## DIFFERENCE BETWEEN A FINANCIAL ADVISOR AND A WEALTH STRATEGIST

In this book you'll see me use the terms "Wealth strategist" and 'Financial advisor" intermittently. Most people believe they characterize the same role but when it comes to managing your finances, there are distinct differences between the two.

A financial advisor typically focuses on providing guidance and assistance with investments, retirement planning, and overall financial management. They analyze your current financial situation, help you set financial goals, and recommend specific investment products such as stocks, bonds, mutual funds, and insurance policies. Their expertise lies in optimizing your portfolio to achieve your financial objectives while considering factors such as risk tolerance, time horizon, and financial constraints.

On the other hand, a wealth strategist takes a broader and more holistic approach to wealth management. They not only address investment strategies but also delve into areas such as tax planning, estate planning, asset protection, and legacy planning. Rather than simply recommending investment products, wealth strategists work to align your financial decisions with your long-term aspirations and values. They focus on optimizing your entire financial picture to create a comprehensive and sustainable wealth plan tailored to your unique circumstances.

While financial advisors specialize in investment management, wealth strategists serve as strategic partners, guiding you through life's financial complexities and helping you make informed decisions that go beyond short-term gains to secure your financial future, legacy, and wealth. Understanding the distinction between these two roles is beneficial as you can know which you need at whatever stage of your financial journey.

Chapter One

# WEALTH EDUCATION FOR YOUR HEIRS

IN THIS CHAPTER, I'LL USE Gerald's story to explain the importance of properly educating your heirs to be great stewards of wealth. He is the grandson of David and Lisa and is an anomaly because normally, a great deal of wealth in America doesn't make it to the third generation. The difference in this family's story is the amount of effort put into educating the next generation about preserving and growing money. The second generation was David Jr. (Gerald's father), and he continued the family's finance education tradition that yielded great fruits in Gerald's life.

## GERALD'S FORTUNE

Gerald had received over $600,000 from his father's life insurance policy, which was earmarked for his own daughter's college tuition. David Jr., his father, had already prepared for the family's fourth generation, which was Gerald's daughter. Gerald decided to put everything he had learned from generations before him into practice. Rather than just waiting with that pile of cash for his daughter to grow to become college-ready, Gerald knew he could do more with that capital than dumping it in a savings account would ever do for him.

He claimed some of the real estate that his father left him and was able to purchase more properties with the $600,000. In the same number of years that it would've taken his daughter to become college-ready, Gerald had amassed a real estate portfolio that was worth about $60 million. He had carefully evaluated the real estate market and built a business around continuously capitalizing on opportunities he spotted.

The value of his real estate portfolio kept soaring. One day as he was discussing with his mentor how he had paid over **$800,000** in taxes, he mentioned how his CPA kept advising him to purchase more cars and more real estate without any long-term strategy in place to keep building and protecting his business and wealth. I remember him narrating the conversation he had with his mentor to me. I remember thinking to myself, "That must be one of the funniest, yet life-changing, conversations you'll ever have with that man." Why? His CPA meant well with his advice, but people who mean well can also harm when they are ill-informed or misinformed. They believe wholeheartedly that the advice they're giving you is true and accurate, but they are not able to tell facts because all they know to be true is misinformation.

I thought the conversation with his mentor was funny because as he narrated the advice he had been receiving from his CPA, his mentor was almost suggesting he take legal action against him! It was that bad. I listened keenly to Gerald's story. After about seven minutes, I couldn't help but burst out laughing! Indeed, his mentor helped him avert what could have been a disaster to his business and wealth.

Gerald was introduced to a wealth strategist who teaches uncommon principles of creating wealth and passing wealth on to the next generation. He contacted this gentleman to set up an initial phone interview. As he sat down and listened to the man speaking on the phone, he realized that the gentleman was more interested in just finding out more about his goals, his wants for his family, his history, and how he meant to improve. Gerald gained more clarity about his future from just one phone call based on the series of questions this man was asking. He was shocked that the man never asked him about how much money he had amassed but instead was asking him questions that made him see his fears as clear as day and see a path forward even brighter than daylight!

Gerald got off that call and sank into deep thought. He was thinking about where he could have been with his business had he met this man even sooner. He considered his mentor's suggestion to pursue legal action against his CPA but reconsidered because he felt that was a bit extreme. While in all this thought, he remembered why he was doing all this—the reasons he had to do better with his money and his business. It wasn't to buy cars and other non-necessities. It wasn't just to make his father, David Jr., proud. It wasn't just to continue the family legacy that his grandparents, David and Lisa, had started. He was more concerned about the future—his daughter, and how to protect the wealth and pass it along just like his grandparents and father had done for him. The wealth of education his father had imparted to him started speaking volumes once more.

At the end of their conversation, the man asked Gerald one final question: *"If you had all the money in the world, what would you like to do?"* Gerald said, *"I'd like to do good and create a family legacy to continue my family's wealth."* The man was intrigued by Gerald's answer and stated what would be the defining theme of their relationship moving forward: *"Your generation will thank you."*

Throughout their conversation, this gentleman had just been taking notes and asking very simple, yet profound, questions. Gerald was surprised that he had never been through this process with any wealth strategist in all his 51 years. The strategist, whom we will name Tony, congratulated Gerald and told him that he had done well based on the background knowledge he already had about finance and building wealth. They had spoken about Gerald's father and grandparents. Tony commended Gerald, telling him that his father had prepared him well. Now, they were going to begin the journey of cementing Gerald's wealth. Tony was determined to make Gerald's dream of doing good and creating a family legacy that continues to make his family wealthy come true.

After three meetings with Tony, they were able to restructure Gerald's entire business portfolio and change the ownership of his company from a single-member limited liability company (LLC) to a multi-member LLC with two partners, with one partner being an irrevocable Complex Business Trust that owned 98 percent of the LLC, while Gerald retained 2 percent ownership. Tony had successfully introduced Gerald to a concept from one of the richest men ever in the world, Mr. John D. Rockefeller: *"Own Nothing, Control Everything."* It was one of the unconventional methods Tony had implemented to get the results he had consistently achieved for his clients for decades. It is also one of the systems elite, super-successful business people have used to protect their wealth for generations. Tony also helped Gerald structure a Private Family Foundation, which is a 501 c3 entity, structured in the form of a Trust, which is one of the keys to creating multi-generational wealth.

Initially, Gerald did not understand the concept, but Tony shared one of his powerful truths to help him understand it more clearly. He said, *"Gerald, we don't own anything naturally. We came to this world empty-handed, and when we die, we sure aren't taking nothing with us."* He explained to Gerald that when you have control as opposed to ownership, you have leverage, flexible decision-making ability, management autonomy, fewer tax burdens, ownership privacy, consolidated assets, simplified estate planning, direct control over asset gifting and transitions, asset protection against personal legal liabilities, clear succession planning, fluid business operations, and many more perks. It started making sense to Gerald. The education he had received about money growing up was fertile ground to receive this new information well.

Gerald was able to donate **$30 million** of personal property, which was already paid off, to a family foundation he had created at Tony's direction, immediately giving him a **$30 million** tax deduction. Tony explained that he did not have to keep buying vehicles like his former CPA had been advising. He also informed Gerald that as the trustee of the foundation, coupled with the fact that he had put all this money inside a property, he could refinance the property, and pull out some of the equity to allow the foundation to begin creating compounding wealth. Gerald had named the foundation after his parents as a tribute to them and in alignment with creating a family legacy and continued generational wealth creation.

Under Gerald's direction, and embedded in the mandate, the foundation supported multiple public charities benefitting the less fortunate. Not only was the foundation's work good for the community and fulfilling for Gerald and his team, but it was also yielding additional significant benefits. He refinanced some of his properties, withdrawing $20,000,000 of equity, and invested in a cash-value life insurance policy, which he max funded with over $1,000,000 a year. The $42,354,934 **total death benefit** was astounding and nearly unbelievable for Gerald who previously thought his investment and wealth prospects had been capped.

The foundation was the owner and the beneficiary of the life insurance contract, a second-to-die policy for him and his wife since they were both trustees of the family foundation. Gerald understood life insurance a little bit but not its true power. He understood that it had helped his father and grandfather successfully park wealth that he and his children would benefit from, but he hadn't explored the liberty to borrow against the policy. Tony introduced him to this system, and Gerald didn't need convincing. He started using his policy as collateral for loans from other financial institutions, to buy shares in startup companies, etc. The profits came back to the foundation tax-free. In less than one year, Gerald doubled his foundation's net worth to $42 million. Regarding the death benefit of his life insurance, it became apparent to him that if he lived for another 40 years, the policy would be worth $132 million. If he lived 10 years more, the death benefit of the policy that will be paid to the foundation would be $258 million, not counting investments that he could make within those timeframes. Gerald also donated to an Ivy League college and created an endowment that pays his family foundation tax-free income for another 15 years.

Gerald's story is not the exception; it is the rule. He was able to set up and protect his wealth because he was educated and connected with the right people who had the right information. He secured his daughter's future and his family legacy firmly, just as wealthy families had done for generations. He implemented Tony's systems, which were instrumental in making all this possible. One critical element is that Gerald remained receptive throughout his relationship with Tony due, in part, to the solid foundation his father had given him to prepare for the wealth he inherited. Gaining knowledge was important. Applying that knowledge proved to be extremely valuable.

This financial education made him less susceptible to luring false financial advice and being enticed to splurge on needless possessions. Gerald may not have had the knowledge that Tony had, but that was okay because he didn't need it. All he needed was the right foundation and someone to point him in the right direction. Super successful business people have taken time to educate their heirs while the wealth isn't yet in their hands, which is the first line of defense for retaining wealth. Without good stewards, it doesn't matter the systems put in place to make money because whoever is in control will tear it down faster than the generations took to painstakingly build it.

Chapter Two

# THE BEST MONEY GARAGES

THE CONCEPT OF MONEY GROWTH must factor in time. One of the reasons people become wealthy is that they've compounded wealth over a good amount of time. Different kinds of wealth require different preservation approaches. They need different storage methods for them to remain in perfect condition. Most perishable valuables should be stored in a secure location, protected from theft or potential external harm, and preserved by different methods to make sure the harm doesn't come from poor maintenance or other oversights.

Money isn't stored like other valuables. For money to retain its value, it cannot be stashed away in a room and locked. Money must be growing and earning more. If not, it is losing value. You shouldn't think of storing money the way you would typically store possessions like houses or cars. I titled this chapter "The Best Money Garages" because I want to talk about the best ways to preserve money while it grows and makes you more money. Any "money garage" you choose must allow your money to grow. Cars stored in garages don't bring in more cars, and that's fine. Money must be allowed to grow. If you have stored money in a money garage that doesn't bring in more money, you have your money in a bad money garage.

Let me tell you a short story about a friend of mine who purchased a three-family unit that he cherished more than most of his other possessions. He had purchased that property as an asset to preserve money secured from several great business deals. It was a great headquarters for his freight business, and he made more money than he needed for his bills and lifestyle. He thought it would be a great idea to "freeze" the money for his children. He had grand plans to keep the property in mint condition, so he devoted time to checking up on his property manager and the job they were doing to ensure every aspect of the property was in tip-top condition. He visited the property almost every week. When he was away on longer trips, he would have his wife keep a keen eye on it to make sure nothing happened that would depreciate the value of their precious three-unit property. He had the lawn pruned and kept the amenities up to date, but all that wouldn't protect him from what the market was about to do to his beloved "asset."

After six years, several buyers started approaching my friend to purchase the property, but he felt insulted by the offers being made. His initial vision for that property was to serve as a garage to store money for the next generation, but he figured he'd entertain offers to learn how the market would value his property after all that time had passed. He had meticulously cared for the property, but market forces beyond his control still dictated its worth.

Real estate is a great investment, although I wouldn't consider it a great option for a money garage. It does not offer competitive returns and it is illiquid, meaning you cannot get your money at will. You also remain at the mercy of market forces that strongly influence the worth of your property.

It's widely preached by many financial advisers that real estate is a great garage to store money, but I have a problem with that because it doesn't have all the characteristics that I seek in one. I teach unconventional methods to store and build wealth that many don't practice. After experiencing several cases with different clients, I've been able to certify that any money garage chosen should meet 12 requirements before you consider putting your money in.

## CHARACTERISTICS OF GREAT MONEY GARAGES

1. **Tax-deferred growth**—Money garages must allow you to defer taxes on interest earned to a future point in time.
2. **Tax-free distribution**—When you want to recoup your money, you should be able to take it out from the garage tax-free.
3. **Competitive return**—The interest rate you earn on the money must be competitive. Inflation should not have negative effects on your money.
4. **High contributions**—You should be able to put as much money as you want into the garage to stockpile.
5. **Deductible contributions**—You should have the liberty to write off contributions made to your money garage.
6. **Collateral opportunities**—Money stored in your money garage should be eligible to be used as collateral for loans.
7. **Safety**—The money garage must guarantee the safety of your money.

8. **No-loss provisions**—You should have guarantees that you will not lose the money you put into the garage.
9. **Guaranteed loan option**—You should be certain of the availability of loans should you need to access money.
10. **Unstructured loan payment**—You should be able to pay back loans at will and on your own time with a structure that's not mandatory.
11. **Liquidity, use, and control**—The money in your garage must be accessible at your discretion and you must have full control over it to do with it as you see fit.
12. **Additional benefits**—There should be benefits that allow you to access your money in case of sickness, emergencies, etc.

When a money garage checks all these boxes, you should strongly consider using it to store wealth for future generations. Real estate checks two of the 12 boxes, but unfortunately, that doesn't qualify it as a great money garage. When a property appreciates with your equity in it, you're accruing interest that you don't pay taxes on; however, if that property is sold, there's no avoiding the taxes that you will be slammed with. You could also use real estate as collateral for loans, which is great. However, those two positives still make real estate pale in comparison to the best money garage.

## THE BEST MONEY GARAGE

When I consider the right place to park cash, this money garage is viable because it passes my personal "garage viability" test by possessing all the characteristics mentioned above.

## CASH-VALUE LIFE INSURANCE

The first-generation heralds of wealth for the family I referenced in Chapter One, David and Lisa, did a fantastic job grooming their son, David Jr. He made use of an exceptional vehicle, which I champion, to its full extent: cash-value life insurance. The possibilities are extensive with this option, including compounding your money over time, while simultaneously borrowing against your policy to start or fund other endeavors.

I've told the story several times of how I borrowed money from my cash-value life insurance to fund my wedding and how my policy is set up in a way that boosts my credit. I have the liberty to structure the payments to ensure I never default as I pay myself back. I do what I need to with the money I take out and enjoy the benefits of having my money earn compound interest at the same time.

No other option gives you the control that a well-structured cash-value life insurance policy offers. Having a stock portfolio, for example, can offer competitive returns, high contributions, liquidity, and guaranteed loan options, but it also has the following downside: the actual amount available is half the value of the stock portfolio; the amount you have available can change subject to federal regulations; loans available to you can fluctuate; and hedge fund shorting could trigger a decline in the underlying security value, which causes margin calls that require cash deposits or a sale of assets in your portfolio. It's not a great money garage!

Banks offer certificates of deposit to customers, which are usually considered safe places to store money, but the downside disqualifies them as great money garages. The interest rates tend to be low, loans must still be negotiated with the banks with no guarantees, and you typically do not have liquidity because the principal committed is subject to a withholding period. Plus, you pay penalties for early withdrawals.

401(k) qualified plans represent another poor garage. I understand why 401(k) plans have been marketed the way they have been over the years. They offer deductible contributions, additional benefits, competitive returns, and tax-deferred growth. However, consider the downside to this garage. Not only are you limited to a maximum of $50,000 loan availability or one-half of the account balance, but loans must also be repaid in five years, or they will be considered as a taxable distribution. In addition, if you are under 59½ years old, you will be charged a 10% early withdrawal penalty. You're also double taxed on loan repayment because the money you used to pay back the loan has been taxed already. Also, a job change triggers loan repayment. Don't forget that layoffs are considered a job change, too, which leaves you at the mercy of your employer.

Life insurance allows your cash to grow tax-deferred. Riders are optional and may be available at an additional cost, but your dividends become guaranteed cash value once they are paid by the insurance company. Loans are a feature of the contract. Also, the contract is unilateral, which means only you have the right to change the provisions. Loans you take out indeed reduce access to available cash value depending on the amount of the loan, but the death benefit is paid income tax-free. It also offers a disability waiver that can pay premiums if the insured is unable to work due to sickness or disability. It is the singular most viable money garage I'd recommend. It is also great because you do not necessarily need regular reviews on your policy. You can even take out a policy for your infant without their involvement, up to the face amount taken out on the principal adult. That means, as a parent taking out insurance on your child, the insurance policy on that child cannot exceed the face amount of the policy that you have on yourself.

I always teach people to never be in a hurry to start investing and to never invest in a trend. The more you stack up your money, the more you will be able to take advantage of other opportunities. With the money he inherited from his father, Gerald could've lived a comfortable lifestyle. He could've taken extensive vacations and made small investments that would've yielded decent returns, but he used the right money garage. Over time, he grew his fortune sheltered from undue taxation and unnecessary fees.

Chapter Three

# FUTURE-PROOFING GENERATIONAL WEALTH

I WOULD LIKE TO BEGIN THIS chapter by sharing one of my favorite Bible verses. I have often heard people talk about wealth like it is a bad element of society. Many preachers have delivered lessons to their congregations about how "*evil*" money and wealth are, or why righteous people shouldn't be concerned about building wealth. When we study to show ourselves approved, we should divide the word of truth rightly.

One Bible verse that is typically used to buttress the idea of wealth being evil is this: "*Lay not up for yourselves treasures upon earth, where moth and rust doth corrupt, and where thieves break through and steal: But lay up for yourselves treasures in heaven, where neither moth nor rust doth corrupt, and where thieves do not break through nor steal: For where your treasure is, there will your heart be also.*"—Matthew 6:19-21

I understand how this verse can be taken literally without further exploration, but when you aim to divide the word and find the truth, you should not isolate text in scripture and draw inaccurate conclusions. This is what I think to myself when I read this verse: "*If I truly believe in a God who sits in heaven and has made the earth His footstool, if I believe God owns all the riches of the earth, all the gold and silver, and all the cattle on a thousand hills, then as His child, why should inheriting my Father's treasures be evil?*" I think that's a fair question to ask.

In my search for an answer, I found a very interesting verse: "*A good man leaves an inheritance to his children's children, But the wealth of the sinner is stored up for the righteous.*"—Proverbs 13:22

This is a complete antithesis to the idea that wealth is evil. I find this verse very interesting because not only does it explain that God's children should indeed be wealthy, but it also articulates:

1. How wealthy God's children should be; and
2. For whom the wealth is designated.

The first verse makes an insightful statement. It says that we shouldn't lay up wealth (treasures) on earth, but the key part of that statement is the subject of *wealth*! It says don't lay up treasures for yourself, which is important because it raises the question of for whom we should be laying up treasures! The second verse has the answer: you should be laying up wealth for your children's children (generational wealth!).

Can you see that God's children shouldn't just be wealthy enough to take care of themselves? The verse even describes "*a good man*" as someone who lays up wealth (treasures) for their children's children. There are a lot of factors that can stop wealth from being passed on across generations. I have dedicated this chapter to addressing how you can future-proof wealth and ensure you are being a good person, according to the Word.

The verse also reiterates what was discussed in Chapter One: that we must shift our perspective of wealth from being owners of wealth to being stewards of wealth. The wealth that I have been blessed with in my lifetime isn't for me. One day I will not be here to enjoy it. I must be extremely prudent and forward-thinking about what comes next.

I remember when I contracted COVID-19 and remained in the hospital for some time. Although I was alone, I was not panicked because I knew I was ready if the worst were to happen. I have been doing everything necessary to ensure a safe and hassle-free wealth transfer because my children and my children's children are the real subjects of my wealth. I see myself as a good steward who is creating this generational wealth for them to grow and steward for future generations! When you have the right wealth education, and shift your mindset from owner to steward, you will see the importance of making sure the wealth is protected and can be successfully transferred.

## FOILING FUTURE ATTACKS

You should live like you're going to die tomorrow and plan like you're going to live forever because you're not in total control of all life's forces. As a good person, you wouldn't want the family wealth to diminish on your watch. Your primary aim would be to grow it, protect it, and successfully transfer it. Many situations are not within our control when it comes to protecting wealth.

There are threats like inflation or an undisciplined family member who cares more about spending than stewarding wealth, but we can anticipate and forestall some of the threats to a family's generational wealth.

When the principal steward of wealth passes on in a family, several things happen. For one, the IRS is standing by to demand an estate tax when properties are to be inherited. The process can be tied up in probate court for years, which will see the family pay undue fees and make the entire process strenuous for everyone involved. Sometimes, an internal family misunderstanding can keep members in court, fighting over who is owed what. Then, when you add the presence of a financial adviser who doesn't have the family's best interests at heart, or who isn't knowledgeable enough about generational wealth, the family's wealth has a slim chance of a successful succession.

I have seen families torn apart by internal feuding. People who love each other, by all accounts, become divided due to varying claims of who deserves what portion of an inheritance. It is common in West Africa, for example, for a misunderstanding to erupt whenever the time comes to *"share property."* There will be claims based on which children add more value to the family business and, thus, deserve more. Several parameters are used to weigh their importance and determine who deserves what. There were cases where the demised would leave "last words" with a trusted confidant, but that was another potential point of dispute because the confidant's word would be contested for validity by those who weren't favored by their claims.

In America, I see wills contested all the time. I see people laying claim to properties based on varying degrees of their perceived deservedness. When it comes to parts of the family's wealth such as businesses, for example, which member of the next generation is most qualified to keep the business afloat? Who is more educated? Who has spent the most time understudying the one to be succeeded? Then there's what is stated in the will and potentially contesting its validity or authenticity. All of these can be avoided if proper succession plans are put in place.

Preparing one's heirs to take over different aspects of the estate is crucial to ensure clear succession exists once the inevitable happens. Wills are good declarations of who gets what aspects of the wealth estate, but without expert assistance in drafting one, they can still be contested and can fail to be a clear blueprint for succession.

Another way to future-proof generational wealth is by setting up impenetrable Trusts with rules. Trusts have several layers of protection that protect a family's wealth from prying elements such as taxation. One such layer is known as irrevocability, which is established by declaration. That means when a piece of property is put into the Trust, and the transfer is declared irrevocable, it is the same as if the property is sold, except there is no tax consequence.

A Trust is an effective way to keep your business and personal wealth protected. The IRS is always lurking around like your silent business partner to see how much of your wealth they can gobble up for themselves, but the Supreme Court has made provisions that even the IRS cannot ignore. The Supreme Court holds that "a trust relationship comes under the realm of Equity Justice based upon the Common Law, and is not subject to legislative restrictions as are corporations and other organizations created by legislative authority."

Having this setup allows you to "own nothing and control everything." Preserving generational wealth has a lot to do with keeping control of assets as opposed to ownership, which is subject to scrutiny and liability. Betting on yourself and setting up your protection is the smarter way to future-proof wealth.

Chapter Four

# SUCCESSFULLY TRANSFERRING WEALTH

THE IDEA OF OWNING A business that can outlive the owner is always attractive. We look at a company like Heinz that was founded by Henry J. Heinz in 1869, over a century ago and is still in business, and wonder how this is possible. Heinz Ketchup was introduced in 1876, passed on to John Heinz (Henry J. Heinz's great-grandson), and has now survived numerous economic downturns, including the recent Great

Recession. In fact, for many of us, it remains our favorite and only ketchup brand. Think of the generations down the line that have benefited and will continue to benefit from this transfer of wealth, including John's widow, Teresa Heinz, who was the immediate successor trustee after his death. The truth is that this sort of transfer of wealth is possible for anyone. You only need to know how it can be done successfully.

Some years ago, I was still learning the ropes in the finance world. I knew very little about Trusts. In one of my presentations, I met an older Black woman who owned a relatively successful Jamaican restaurant in America. She was sold on the idea of getting a life insurance policy to create and transfer her wealth to her children. She consulted me and purchased a life insurance policy for $300,000 in death benefits at a premium of $200 a month. It was a term insurance policy for 20 years. As the story goes, less than three years later, she died. She had four children and made three of them beneficiaries.

She did not include her first daughter, who was married, and whom she felt was quite successful. Instead, she made her the executor of her estate. After the woman's death, I got a call from the first daughter asking me to file a claim on the policy, given that I was her mother's agent. Immediately, I called the insurance company to find out the details of the beneficiaries. Somehow, her name had not been included as a beneficiary of this insurance policy. I had to relay this information to her, and I could see the obvious shock and disappointment written all over her face when she found out what her mother had done. It meant she would not get paid any money from the death benefits.

At the time the owner consulted me to get the life insurance policy, I had, indeed, suggested making her first daughter a beneficiary. After all, she was doing pretty well with her independent business, but the mother declined.

After her death, the daughter, being the executor of the estate, would now have to employ the services of lawyers and endure probate court proceedings at the expense of her business because her mother did not leave behind a Will or Trusts. At the same time, she would not get a cent from the life insurance policy benefits, which did not need a probate court. Her siblings enjoyed these benefits, unfortunately. Even worse, the restaurant business died subsequently after the owner died because her siblings cared very little for it and would not assist her with any money to sustain its day-to-day operations.

Honestly, I blame myself for how things unfolded in the aftermath of the woman's death. Yet, I was quick to admit that I was young and inexperienced at the time.

Moving forward, I made a promise to myself to never let such a mess happen again. I could have advised this woman better if I had known better. Well-structured Trusts and a beneficiary list would have preserved this woman's business for generations.

Also, I learned that a very important way to preserve wealth for the incoming generation is to objectively identify the true heirs to your business and ensure they get the requisite financial education. It is important to treat each child as an employee, with the understanding that they each have their strengths and weaknesses. You must analyze your children's strengths carefully and patiently, especially based on how they treat money and their knack for leadership. Simple money habits like saving a good chunk of their monthly allowances to buy nice toys for themselves, instead of spending frivolously and then asking for more, can point you to which of them will be interested in an opportunity to work in your company, and eventually take over as successor. Remember that each child is different and possesses unique abilities. You may broaden your scope to members of your extended family. In the end, the aim is to continue the family legacy and preserve the wealth for generations.

The implications of a lazy and unobjective identification of your heirs and a poorly structured Trust are not just hatred and lengthy legal battles within the family, but gross mismanagement of the wealth you strategically amassed while alive—A case in point is the story of Lisa Marie Presley. The popular American songwriter's dad, Elvis Presley, left her a huge inheritance. Yet, years after she became Trustee of the estate, the Trust had been reduced to $14,000 in cash and $500,000 in credit card debt. When Lisa died, it took seven months and numerous court petitions and disputes before her first daughter, Riley Keough was named the sole Trustee of her estate.

I began researching super-successful families. I changed my mentor circle. In truth, it formed the motivation for writing my first book, *Creating Generational Wealth: What the Super-Wealthy Know that You Need to Know®*.

Now, to better understand what I am about to teach you, I advise you to get the book alongside this one if you have not read it.

A life insurance policy is an important vehicle for creating wealth that can be transferred to the next generation. But to take full advantage of this policy, especially if your net worth is above $75,000, you need a Trust. Please note that a Trust is different from a Will. The differences are extensively covered in my book,

*Creating Generational Wealth: What the Super-Wealthy Know that You Need to Know®*.

Two important advantages Trusts have over Wills are time and Guardianship planning. Essentially, this means that the business can be transferred naturally without being easily challenged in court, and a court guardian is not needed when you are deceased. A properly structured Trust can prevent your heirs or beneficiaries from paying additional money after your death due to liability or taxes.

## WHAT IS A TRUST?

A Trust is a fiduciary relationship where one party (the Trustor) transfers the right of ownership of properties or assets to hold on behalf of and for the benefit of a third party. They are established to provide legal protection for the Trustor's assets and ensure that the assets are distributed according to the Trustor's wishes. A Trustor transfers assets to a Trustee for the benefit of the beneficiary.

In the United States, Title 26 of the US Code Section 6012 sub a, sub 4, identifies a Trust as a separate and distinct taxable person. In other words, according to the U.S. government, a Trust can do everything a human being can do except talk, eat, breathe, or perform other biological functions. This is how powerful a fiduciary Trust is.

There are over 80 different types of Trusts, but for the sake of this book, I'll help you know how super-wealthy individuals use well-structured, complex Trusts to hold business and family assets.

To help you understand this concept properly, let us continue with the story of David and Lisa, who were able to successfully build and transfer wealth to David Jr., who then stewarded this wealth and passed it on to his son, Gerald, and his wife.

Gerald, through the advice of Tony, had successfully compounded the inherited wealth and established a Trust to efficiently preserve his wealth for his wife and daughter.

Tony advised Gerald to convert his single-member Limited Liability Company (LLC) to a multi-member LLC to protect his assets. Only the members can be taxed on distributed income. An agreement had also been reached in the LLC, where Gerald gets only two percent of whatever income is made by the multi-member LLC, while 78 percent ownership of the LLC is transferred to the Business Trust. The remaining 20 percent goes to the Family Foundation. While Gerald is alive, he is the Trustee. Upon his death, his wife will become the Successor Trustee since there was no prenuptial agreement.

During one year, the multi-member LLC grossed $10 million in revenue. Five million dollars, which were taxed, had been spent on employee salaries and other expenses, leaving a net income of $5 million. Remember that Gerald is a partner of the LLC with 2% ownership, and will only get 2 percent of the net income. Therefore, only $100,000 was paid to his account. Twenty percent of the net profit, or $1 million, went to the charitable foundation. The remaining 78 percent—$3.9 million—was transferred to the Business Trust.

This important decision reduced Gerald's possible exposure to lawsuits. For instance, if Gerald were to go through a divorce with his wife, or be sued by his creditors, either of these parties could only lay claim to a portion of the $100,000 in his account. Do you remember the quote by John D. Rockefeller that I referenced in Chapter One—"Own nothing, control everything?" That is the key to wealth!

## WHAT IS A BUSINESS TRUST?

In the United States, a Business Trust conducts business privately and pays taxes on profits through a 1041 tax form. Only the Trustees can distribute benefits to the beneficiaries. For Gerald, his Family Trust is the beneficiary of the profits made by the Business Trust. The Trustee controls the affairs of a Trust, including credit cards and bank accounts. For instance, whenever Gerald goes on business trips or uses the business's private jet, the Business Trust incurs these expenses. In simpler terms, whatever a Trust owns is an expense to the Trust. The Trust also distributes forms to its contractors for expenses paid to them, representing earned income. The details are sent to the Internal Revenue Service to ensure that the Trust and the contractors share the tax burden.

### Gerald's Business Trust

The Business Trust received $3.9 million from the Multi-member LLC. Gerald had taken business trips. The trust procured properties and invested in companies. These expenses cost the Trust $1.9 million. To continue to reduce liabilities, the Business Trust distributed the remaining $2 million to the Family Trust via a K-1 form.

## WHAT IS A FAMILY TRUST?

The Family Trust, like the Business Trust, conducts its private affairs and takes all its allowed deductions. It also pays taxes on any amount remaining after taking all allowable deductions. Allowable deductions are expenses deducted from taxable income to reduce taxes paid. For example, a Family Trust can donate to a charitable Foundation. Charitable donations cannot be taxed by the government.

### Gerald's Family Trust

Gerald was advised by Tony to transfer the ownership of his house and other assets within it to the Family Trust via a Quitclaim deed. The Family Trust pays the mortgage, utility bills, groceries, Life Insurance, and other expenses. Technically, he did not own anything, even as little as a piece of cutlery. The cars he and his wife drive are owned by the Family Trust.

The Family Trust is the owner and beneficiary of the Life Insurance Policy. The insurance premium became an expense for the Trust, and at the same time, it will receive the death benefits when Gerald or his successors die. All these expenses amounted to $1 million. The Family Trust donated $1 million to the Charity Foundation established by Gerald's Family Trust, which he named in tribute to his parents. Do not forget that the goal is to limit liabilities as much as possible while compounding wealth.

## DEFERRED SALES TRUST

A Deferred Sales Trust is similar to Family and Business Trusts in its goal to limit liabilities but with a few complexities. It is a contract between an investor and a third-party Trust (usually unrelated to the investor) in which the property of the investor is sold to the Trust with the payment mode already determined and for a specific period. These payments are called installments.

The reason many investors opt for a Deferred Sales Trust is to defer capital gains tax over time. They are an alternative to 1031 exchanges, where investors can defer taxation by swapping their real estate and investing the returns in similar or "like-kind" properties. Unlike 1031 exchanges, a Deferred Sales Trust can defer capital gains tax indefinitely. The Federal government deducts 20 to 35% on properties sold at a long-term profit relative to its cost. Hence, by utilizing a Deferred Sales Trust, investors can defer the payment of this charge indefinitely.

The working of this Trust is the method of payment, which is in installments. The capital gains in a Sales Deferred Trust are calculated using the gross profit ratio. The gross profit ratio is the profit that would have been earned were it to be paid as a lump sum instead of in installments.

Let's work with the story of Gerald to give you a practical understanding of how to effectively utilize a Deferred Sales Trust.

Gerald was going to sell one of the properties willed to him by his father, David Jr., to purchase a similar kind of property. However, after consulting with Tony, his wealth strategist, Gerald was advised to transfer the ownership of the property to his Trust, who could now sell it on his behalf. The estate was worth $400,000 at the time David Jr. acquired it. The Trust sold it for $800,000. The capital gains or gross profit on the investment was $400,000. The gross profit ratio was calculated as the gross profit divided by the selling price: $400,000/$800,000 = 0.5. If the Trust had agreed with Gerald to pay him $200,000 in income from the sale of the property for two years, the capital gain per year would come to $100,000 (0.5 × $200,000). Assuming the tax rate on the capital gain is 20% ($80,000), Gerald would owe $20,000 annually in capital gain taxes.

Instead, following Tony's advice, Gerald's Trust decided to defer the capital gain tax indefinitely. The trust opted to invest the $800,000 from the sale of the estate in the shares of profitable businesses, from which he would now be paid the dividends annually. Gerald avoided paying taxes indefinitely on the sale of his inherited estate.

## LEVERAGING A CHARITABLE FOUNDATION TO PRESERVE WEALTH

The first important note to make is that Charitable Foundations are not regulated by any civil agency. Their assets are not taxable because the community benefits from the activities of the foundation. They are autonomous entities that may own assets and engage in profitable business ventures for maximum yields.

The Foundations may own up to 20% equity in other businesses. They are only required to donate a minimum of 5% of their assets every year. The Charitable Foundation was created by the Family Trust. Therefore, the Trustees of the Family Trust determine the investments of the Charitable Foundation. Examples of these kinds of grant-donating foundations include the Oprah Winfrey Foundation, the Bill and Melinda Gates Foundation, the Rockefeller Foundation, etc.

For Gerald, his Private Family Foundation, having received the $1 million as a donation from the Family Trust, spent $500,000 on its operating expenses, including employees' salaries. From its net donation, it donated the minimum required five percent ($25,000). The Charity Foundation, on instruction from Gerald as the Trustee, used the retained balance ($475,000) for alternative investments to continue growing the Foundation's wealth. He asked to meet with his wealth strategist, Tony, who advised him to commit $500,000 for a single-premium Whole Life Insurance policy as a 55-year-old instead of depositing it into a traditional savings account. This type of Insurance policy is used for legacy transfers. In effect, Gerald will not have to pay any more premiums. The death benefit of this policy is $1 million. The advantage of this policy is that Gerald may access the cash surrender value at any point or take a loan against the value.

The Foundation, from previous annual profits, committed another $1 million to purchase an Index Universal Life Policy worth $34 million in death benefit. The Foundation will pay $1 million annually in subsequent years. The Foundation also considered using $1.7 million from other business profits to add to this policy as the maximum possible premium.

These are the raw numbers of this policy:

- At an annual premium of $1 million for the Index Universal Life policy, Gerald's Foundation will be paid a death benefit of $70,265,914 if Gerald lives up to age 80. This means that $1 million for 26 years—that is, $26 million, would guarantee a return of over $70 million at death while having a cash value of $36,265,914.

- At the maximum allowed premium of $2.7 million annually, if he were to die at age 80, his Foundation would get a death benefit of $181,933,476 while having a cash value of $147,933,476.
- At age 90, the death benefit at the maximum allowed premium compounds to $326,076,103 tax-free.

Wealthy individuals know the importance of living a long life. Hence, they make a healthy lifestyle their priority. You only need to look at wealthy men like Warren Buffet (93), and Bill Gates (67) who are still living beyond the average American life expectancy. This is how the wealthy stay wealthy!

Interestingly, the Rockefellers, Carnegies, and several other super-wealthy families in the early 1900s began their Foundations in response to the introduction of the income tax by the U.S. government in 1913. These families, according to investigations by the commission created by the 62nd Congress, sought to control large aspects of the economy like education and social services through their foundations instead of their employees.

You can see that this vehicle for transferring wealth successfully has existed for a long time. The super-wealthy families do not only care about creating and compounding wealth; they seek knowledge on how to successfully preserve the wealth with the following objectives:

1. Treating the children fairly;
2. Choosing a fitting heir to control the business while others have equity and benefit from the growing value; and
3. Ensuring the assets are passed on to future generations without any reduction in estate value.

Engaging a wealth strategist and taking advantage of a Family Trust, a Business Trust, and a Private Family Foundation, as Gerald did, are guaranteed ways to fulfill these objectives and transfer wealth successfully.

In the next chapter, I will further discuss two types of cash-value Life Insurance Policies and how they may be used to preserve generational wealth while being driven by Trusts.

Chapter Five

# WHOLE LIFE VS. INDEX UNIVERSAL LIFE FOR PRESERVING GENERATIONAL WEALTH

IN CHAPTER TWO, I EXPLAINED the concept and need for "money garages" to help grow and preserve your wealth. Make no mistake, this is how super-wealthy families think of money and opportunities. I also emphasized the characteristics you must seek in a money garage. For every money garage I choose, it must undergo the "garage viability test."

Eight very important characteristics of money garages that will form the foundation of what I am about to teach you are:

1. Tax-deferred growth, which allows you to defer tax on future interest earned
2. Competitive returns that are not impacted by inflation
3. Liquidity
4. Uninterrupted compounding interest
5. Collateral capacity
6. Full control
7. Opportunity cost
8. Tax-free distribution in the form of loans

With this knowledge, we can delve deeper into the ever-amazing world of Cash-Value Insurance. Here, I will explain the concepts and application of Whole Life Insurance and Index Universal Life Insurance policies for investors and Infinite Banking. You will learn which is ideal for you. I will teach you the intricacies of these policies as an expert with over two decades of experience in the finance industry. I have walked in your shoes, owning over 20 Life Insurance policies already.

If, at some point, you have consulted an insurance agent on life insurance policies, the chances are that Whole Life Insurance and Index Universal Life Insurance policies must have been dangled before you. In fact, in a bid to convince you on which to opt for, these advisors must have told you that this is the secret to the generational wealth of top global companies like Disney and JCPenney. They are partly correct.

According to Walt Disney's Disneyland sourcebook, Walt Disney took advantage of the Whole Life Insurance policy to invest in Disney World when traditional banks snubbed him. JCPenney utilized the same kind of policy to pay his employees after the stock market crashed in 1929. This plan has existed for decades. On the other hand, Index Universal Life Insurance was introduced to the market less than 20 years ago. Those companies did not use the Index Universal Life policy when their financial challenges arose because it had not been developed.

I own Whole Life and the Index Universal Life policies. They are excellent policies that provide cash value for their owners. In other words, their benefits are tax-free. However, based on their peculiarities, one is more ideal for a particular situation than the other.

Whole Life Insurance exists effectively as a replacement for a savings account, a money market account, or a Certificate of Deposit. It is a fixed account with no flexibility, and the returns (interest rate) are guaranteed.

Most clients would treat a Whole Life Insurance policy as an emergency savings account because it allows immediate access to your cash if properly structured, with no time limitations using "paid-up additions." Paid-up additions are small bits of Whole Life Insurance purchased with the dividends of the policy. This means you can use dividends from your Whole Life policy to purchase small packs of Life Insurance. The aim is to keep increasing the coverage and value of your Whole Life Insurance while being able to surrender them for cash value as well as using them as collateral for loans.

The major difference between a Whole Life Insurance policy and a common savings account is that it gives protection on your life (coverage) while paying a considerably higher interest rate than a traditional bank.

Index Universal Life insurance (IUL), on the other hand, provides an often better option than the Thrift Savings Plan (TSP), 401(k), and ROTH IRA. This policy provides benefits like these products but with even more convenience and potential advantages. IUL interest rates are impacted by the forces of the market but are not tied to the market. Hence, the returns are conservative. When the S&P 500 Index drops, you don't lose a penny, but your gains increase as the market grows. I call it the long-term player. They are better used for long-term savings.

For example, if John, a 45-year-old senior developer at a fintech company, earns an annual gross income of $500,000, and his income tax is 35 percent ($175,000), his net income becomes $325,000. If John decides to save in his company's 401(k) account, he's only allowed to contribute a maximum of $22,500 as of 2023. If John dies before the end of the year, his family will likely need the services of an attorney and a probate court to gain access to his money.

As a high-income earner and an accredited investor who has earned more than the allowed $200,000 for more than two years, John just does not find this plan attractive. Another option would be a Whole Life Insurance policy for $150,000 with a death benefit of $1 million at a compounding four percent interest rate.

Instead, John plays the long-term game and opts for an IUL Insurance policy and funds it with a maximum of $150,000 with a death benefit of $2,588,925. As a smart investor, John funded this policy through his Private Foundation that he set up three years ago. He donated 30 percent ($150,000) of his gross income of $500,000 to the Foundation, through which he purchased his IUL Insurance policy. His taxes of 34 percent could only be deducted from the remaining balance of $350,000, which is his gross income minus his charity donation.

Now that you understand the differences between the Whole Life and the Index Universal Life Insurance policies, I can successfully teach you how to use a Trust as the driver of these vehicles to grow and preserve your wealth for future generations.

Let's continue with Gerald's brilliant story to give you a practical understanding.

As Gerald continued to grow his wealth using his Trust, Life Insurance policies, and other investments, he knew that it was time to begin planning for their newborn daughter, Kimberly. He consulted Tony once again. At Tony's instruction, Gerald's Trust, worth over $34 million, purchased an Index Universal Life Insurance Policy for baby Kimberly with a coverage of $2 million at a maximum premium rate of $28,000 annually. This formed another smart parking garage for Gerald.

This was a brilliant financial decision because, instead of purchasing a house in Kimberly's name, like a financial adviser might have otherwise advised, he chose to get a Life Insurance package. For instance, a $2 million house mortgage at a 5 percent interest rate would have cost Gerald $10,736 monthly or $128,832 annually. Yet, when Kimberly turns 30, the cash value of her Index Universal Life Insurance policy will be $2,530,372, and the death benefit worth $6,325,930, both of which are owned by the Family Trust.

As Kimberly grew older, Gerald also began educating her on growing and preserving wealth.

Unfortunately, at age 61, Gerald died of a cardiac arrest. Kimberly was only 19 years old. The Trust, which had become the owner of Gerald's Life Insurance policy, laid a claim to his death benefits of $51,283,636. Gerald, while alive, had agreed with the Trust to pay Kimberly an annual salary of $100,000 while she studied Business and Strategic Investment in college.

Five years later, Kimberly had completed college and was dating her boyfriend, Franklyn. They decided to get married the following year. The Trustee visited Kimberly and her boyfriend in their rented apartment to inform them of the decision to get 21-year-old Franklyn an Index Universal Life Insurance package worth $2,053,218 in coverage at an annual premium of $57,735. Franklyn, who was aware of his girlfriend's Life Insurance policy and the annual wage she received following her dad's demise, agreed to the deal. The Trust was now in control of $5,082,533 as Life Insurance coverage for Kimberly and Franklyn.

If, hypothetically, they both died in an accident on the same day, the Trust would be able to claim their death benefits of $5,082,533. However, with each year the couple is alive, the cash value of the insurance policy continues to appreciate. Remember, at age 19, the death benefit of Kimberly's IUL had appreciated and was now worth $3,029,315. Remember, the Trust is both the owner and the beneficiary of the policy.

Meanwhile, Kimberly, owing to the financial education she received from her dad, purchased for herself a Whole Life Insurance policy worth $2 million at an annual maximum premium of $50,000. This would serve as an emergency savings account. She could fund this plan from the $400,000 salary she earned annually as a Chief Financial Officer at a top bank in the United States.

Two years after they had been married, Kimberly became pregnant, giving birth to a son, Giannis. Just before Giannis celebrated his first birthday, the Trustee met with Kimberly and Franklyn. They increased Kimberly's annual salary to $150,000 to enable her and her husband to cater to their newborn. The Trust also purchased an Index Universal Life Insurance Policy for Giannis worth $2 million in coverage at a $33,315 annual premium. The implication is that when Giannis turns 28, the cash value of his policy will have grown significantly, and if by good fortune he lives to be 100 years old, his Index Universal Life Insurance policy will have grown to a sum of $321,538,749 tax-free in death benefits, which will be paid to the Trust as death benefits when he eventually passes on. His children will also get annual salaries like his mother, Kimberly, did.

When Giannis turned five, Kimberly and Franklyn agreed to have another child. Stephanie was born. As had become the norm, The Trustee administrator visited the family, increased Kimberly's annual salary to $200,000, and purchased an Index Universal Life Insurance Policy for Stephanie. The coverage of the insurance policy was $2 million at a premium of $28,000 annually. When Stephanie turns 28, her Index Universal Life Insurance policy will be worth $2,166,152 in cash value and $5,003,059 in death benefit.

Gerald's singular decision to utilize the Trust in driving his insurance policies meant that the financial future of two generations after him was fully secured. His daughter did not have to start from scratch, and neither did her husband and children.

While Gerald unfortunately passed on, the Trust is bound to exist for life. In the same vein, the Trust's decision to purchase the Index Universal Life Insurance policies meant that they could earn returns in the long term without the burden of taxes and risks. Kimberly could also quickly access the funds independently and tax-free using her well-structured Whole Life Insurance Plan that she purchased at 19.

The super-wealthy families, as I have observed, know that the surest way to grow and preserve wealth is to ensure that the value of their investments is not affected by economic downturns and by limiting their liabilities, especially taxes. As a result, these cash-value policies are solid vehicles to continue transferring wealth across generations.

Chapter Six

# LIFE SETTLEMENTS TO GROW WEALTH

WHEN YOU THINK OF Deutsche Bank, Blackstone, or Berkshire Hathaway, you recognize a common denominator between them: they are top institutional investors. But even more, there are concepts for growing wealth that they have in common. This is what gives them the edge and ensures that they continue to remain in the one percent of wealthy institutions forever. This is what I will teach you in this chapter. I promise you it will blow your mind!

The most common advice many people receive when they consult financial advisers on investments is to put their money in real estate and stocks. To be clear, there is nothing technically wrong with investing in real estate, buying stocks, and regularly monitoring the S&P 500 market. However, as I said in Chapter Two, the returns on investment in real estate are not competitive or guaranteed. Real estate is not readily liquid and relies on the forces of the market when you need to find a buyer later. These investments certainly will not pass my garage viability test.

From my observation of wealthy individuals in the last two decades, one thing I have uncovered is that they value the concept of time. It is the single most powerful concept in life. It is their biggest currency. When they think of investment, they think of it in terms of the scarcity of time—how long it will take to get returns and how long it will take to recover their money if they lose it. Therefore, they are constantly in search of guarantees.

It is funny hearing some financial advisers say that wealthy individuals take the biggest risks with their investments. I have found this to be quite untrue. What wealthy people do better than anyone else is they take well-calculated risks while being optimistic. They are always looking to eliminate as many unnecessary risks as possible. They want to know their returns on investments and the time it will take to fully yield those returns. That is why they spend huge amounts of money on quality research to enable them to make accurate predictions. The stock market, on the contrary, is built on speculation.

The wealthy are always out to nullify the quote by Benjamin Franklin, "Nothing is certain except death and taxes."

One excellent money garage is Life Settlements. A Life Settlement is a form of alternative investment. The fantastic thing about this garage is that it has become open to wealthy individual investors only in the last few years. This makes what I am about to teach you more profound. In the beginning, Life Settlements were only available to institutional investors. But now, individual investors with foresight can capture institutional profits through Life Settlements.

Another great feature of Life Settlements is that individuals who live outside the United States, for example, can invest in Life Settlements in the U.S. through the secondary markets. What I mean is that, just like some wealthy Africans come to the United States to invest in real estate, they can consult wealth strategists like me and get Life Settlements with guaranteed returns, regardless of what happens in the stock market. Did you know that most of the investors on Wall Street do not just invest on Wall Street?

Now, before we go on, it is important to answer one recurring question I have consistently been asked since I became a wealth strategist—one I suspect you might now be pondering as you read this book: "Why should I trust insurance companies with my money?"

I will answer this question with a few well-researched facts. According to *Time* magazine, there are more assets in U.S. Insurance companies than all the world banks combined. An A- or better-rated company can have every client die simultaneously and still be able to pay all the claims. Their reserves are "100 percent real." That's how buoyant insurance companies are. No wonder Bank of America has $8.6 billion in real estate assets, yet has $21.7 billion in Life Insurance cash value, which is calculated to be 10 percent of the Bank's total equity capital. Wells Fargo, similarly, has $18.4 billion in Life Insurance cash value, worth 12 percent of its total equity capital, compared with $8.5 billion owned as real estate assets. These financial institutions know what most people do not know about the immense benefits of investing in Insurance companies.

Another question you might ask is, "Why should I invest my money in a Life Settlement?"

To answer this question, I'll first share with you the conclusion of a study done by the University of Pennsylvania's Wharton Business School in 2002. The study examined 1,584 policies and found that the average "cash surrender value" was $98.4 million, while the average "Life Settlement" from these policies was $336.3 million. This means that the combined owners of these policies earned more than three times in selling as a Life Settlement than what they would have been paid if they had surrendered (canceled) their policies. In other words, the Life Settlement option provided seniors with $240 million they would have otherwise lost if they had accepted the cash surrender value.

In the last four years, Life Settlements have provided more than $8 billion in additional value to citizens in America alone. You can take a fair guess at how much institutional investors would have made in expected returns from their Life Settlements in the years 2019, 2020, and 2021 when the COVID pandemic shook the entire world economy. The sad truth is that lots of seniors with characteristically low immunity lost their lives because of being in the high-risk group of people vulnerable to the disease.

The CEO of the Blackstone Group, Stephen A. Schwarzman, is regarded as one of the 40 most powerful people in finance by Forbes. He is known as a man "too smart to fail." He continues winning through financial downturns and crises. In 2000, when the internet stocks crashed and Alan Greenspan's Federal Reserve had begun lowering interest rates, Schwarzman was perfectly positioned to take advantage of this crisis by investing in alternative investments that offered returns that were not linked to the stock market.

In early 2014, Blackstone paid $100 million in Life Settlement policies to earn a guaranteed return of $800 million in face value. Later that same year, Blackstone invested $100 million in Life Settlements for a return of $1.13 billion in face value. By the middle of the following year, Schwarzman's company had paid $385 million in Life Settlements to earn a guaranteed payout of $1.8 billion.

At the end of 2015, Schwarzman had moved up the pecking order on Wall Street as the "most powerful banker on the planet," ahead of bankers at JP Morgan and Goldman Sachs.

It might also interest you to know that Berkshire Settlements Incorporated, owned by one of the richest men in the world, Warren Buffet, is one of the leading providers of Life Settlements in the United States. Berkshire Settlements Inc. is a member of the Life Insurance Settlement Association (LISA), which is the oldest and largest organization representing players in the Life Settlement industry. Berkshire Settlements Incorporated commits **$600 million** annually to the business.

At this juncture, the question to ask is, "Why not Life Settlements?"

## WHAT IS A LIFE SETTLEMENT?

A Life Settlement is the sale of an already existing insurance policy to a third party for a one-time payment. Seniors who have insurance policies that they no longer need or cannot afford can sell them for more than their cash value and less than their face value. They sell these policies without lapsing or surrendering them. In simpler terms, they foreclose their policies. The purchaser of this policy becomes the beneficiary of the policy and will receive the death benefits when the insured dies.

Depending on where the Life Settlement is purchased, the purchaser might need to continue paying the premiums, otherwise called the "call premium," or in other cases, the premiums might be deducted from the cash value of the policy. This happens when the policy is bought directly from the **Life Settlement** company. On the other hand, if you buy a policy through a hedge fund, what you get is based on a rate of return. They calculate the rate of return to be paid as a percentage of the death benefit for a fixed number of years. This is usually dependent on the life expectancy of the insured. They sell that same policy to multiple people because they aim to continually make money.

A Life Settlement is usually a win-win for every party involved—well, except for the insurance companies, who prefer their clients to cancel or walk away from their policies. The reason, of course, is that they never enjoy paying out death benefits.

However, seniors who might need the money to take care of themselves after retirement or even pay huge hospital bills can get access to quick cash just by selling their insurance policies. The settlements are also higher than if they canceled their plans. At the same time, individual or institutional investors can also get quite competitive and guarantee returns from these policies within a short period. Their returns are not dependent on the S&P 500 market or any economic downturns.

One of the reasons many investors delved heavily into the secondary market for Life Settlements was because of the financial crisis that occurred between 2007 and 2009, where the S&P 500 market was off 53 percent from its October peak, seeing its worst six-month drop in percentage terms (42.7 percent) since 1932 when it dropped 45.4 percent in six months. The Dow Jones Industrial fell six months consecutively, more than 50 percent off its record highs hit in October 2007.

## HOW A LIFE SETTLEMENT WORKS

The Life Settlement transaction is modeled after a real estate transaction. It ends in a change of ownership from the existing owner to the new owner, with closing documents. It works almost like a zero-coupon bond, where the purchaser knows what the expected return on the Life Settlement will be. There is no guesswork. The purchaser does not need to know the happenings on the stock market front. The policies are purchased at a discount to the face value of the death benefit. An individual investor can invest in Life Settlements through their cash accounts, 401(k) rollover, entities, self-directed IRAs, and even Trusts.

In terms of technicalities, the difference between buying a Life Insurance policy and a Life Settlement is time. For Life insurance policies, the higher the life expectancy, the higher the expected returns. However, for Life Settlements, the shorter the life expectancy, the better the investment.

## GERALD'S LIFE SETTLEMENT INVESTMENT

To provide you with a real-life understanding of the workings of a Life Settlement, I will once again use the story of Gerald and how his Trust grew and preserved wealth using this policy.

Gerald's Charity Foundation annually receives an agreed-upon 20 percent of the net income made by his Multi-member LLC. The Foundation donated a minimum of 5 percent to charity after deducting its expenses. The retained balance was used in alternative investments to grow the Foundation's wealth.

In one of the financial years, Gerald's Foundation, in consultation with Tony, his wealth strategist, decided to invest in a Life Settlement. They delved into the secondary market and purchased a life settlement policy for $368,107 with a face value of $500,000 at a 35.83 percent return. The Foundation did not go through Hedge Funds; hence, they had 100 percent ownership of the policy. The age of the policy owner was 83 at the time of underwriting, and he had a life expectancy of 43 months.

Please note that insurance companies invest in actuaries, who can utilize statistics and financial theory to measure and manage risks and uncertainties. Life insurance actuaries develop policies for groups and individuals by creating estimates of how long a person will live.

If, between the day of the purchase and 43 months, the policy owner dies, Gerald's Charity Foundation will get a guaranteed total payout of $500,000. Indeed, if the man were to die the following day after transferring ownership, the Foundation would still get the full payout. They would simply have to wait. Their money was going to work for them.

This is precisely how a Life Settlement works. It is a guaranteed way to grow wealth for future generations without any links to the activities of the stock market. This is the priceless information that wealthy individuals have that keeps them in the one percent forever.

# THANK YOU!

THERE IS A FAMOUSLY SPOKEN phrase in Nigeria, where I grew up, which in more ways than one has helped me soar in my different endeavors: "It takes a community to raise a child." And in many ways, ideas are nurtured like children.

In birthing and successfully articulating the idea to put this book together—*Preserving Generational Wealth: Why the One Percent Never Start from Scratch and How to Give Your Heirs the Same Edge*—a lot of my colleagues have been immensely supportive. For your impact, I say a huge THANK YOU!

## In no particular order:

Tanesha R Abass
Robert F Abercrombie
Anthony D Abrams
Chuck N Abuadinma
Monique Y Abujana
Joana Achanfuo Yeboah
Sonia D Adams
Valerie R Adams
Adebayo A Adebowale
Omowunmi B Adedokun
Adedayo Adeoye
Oladipupo Adesina
Wilhelmina L Adesoye
Abidemi Adetutu
Babajide O Adetutu
Oladapo Adeyale
James Afueh
Ayomide S Agbayewa
Olumide E Agbayewa
Philip A Ager
Lisa L Agoba
Farrakh Ahmed
Oluwole Ajagbe
Fatima O Ajao
Norman D Alday
Mario A Alfaro
Amir M Ali
Razan A Ali
Mitchell Alkins
Shaenee S Allaire
Corashia D Allen-Hicks
Marpessa D Allen
Tangela L Allen
Yolanda Almodovar
Yetunde O Aloba
Michele D Alston
Tonya M Alvarez
Mary O Ama
Jennifer L Ames

William H Ames
Eddie Amoah
Melinda K Amos
Oheneba K Amponsah
Jean-Robert Anantua
LaShanda
Anderson-Love
Bonnie L Anderson
Breona K Anderson
Carl W Anderson
David G Anderson
Gregory L Anderson
Marie L Andre
Alexis Andrews
Rodney J Andrews
Cantrell M Andrews
Tiara Y Andrews
Kalenda A Anglen
Maurice A Anichebe
Levi O Anigwe
Jesse P Annett
Nana C Ansah
Carolyn Aquis
Laciana N Arrington
Barimah
Asare-Dwamenah
Benita L Ashford
Ebenezer A Ashitei
Jacob A Ashitey
Evans O Asiago
Christine Assefa
Onika J Assing
Cathy M Atkins
Jean J Atkins
Andrea H Atkinson
Kwami A Attipoe
Evaline K Atuti
Hans Augustin
Shardae H Avents

Theresa D Ayise
Joseph T Ayuk
Babatunde Bada
Jocelyn S Bagley
Mohamed Bah
Bianka A Bailey
F A Bailey
Jerry D Bailey
Maurice Bailey
Monica L Baker
Saran T Baker
Melissa U Balcombe
Celeste M Baldwin
Jaynefrances W Baldwin
Randolph Ballard
Bankflow Empire Fina
Derrick T Banks
Joel D Banks
Kenneth A Banks
Nathaniel C Banks
Shanicia Bannis
Amberleigh M Barb
Havis T Bardouille
Stephanie A Barimah
Kamilah Barker
Shanice A Barker
Dana B Barnes
Lisa G Barnes
Tamara N Barnes
Vera Barnes
Jewell L Barnett
Pearl Barnwell
Kenya Barry
Empra V Bass
Danita M Batteau
Charlene L Battle
Quentin N Battle
Sumaiyah A Bayan
Kenneth M Beath

Dominique D Beatty
Joseph Beatty
Jennifer C Beaujour
Anthony R Beharry
Monique Beidleman
Felicia L Bell
Jazmine L Bell
John P Bell
Laura Bella
Antoine Bellamy
James R Bellamy
Niquia S Benford
Sabrina L Benjamin-Bailey
Alii Saadi Benn Bey
Egzabia L Bennett
Kerry-Ann T Bennett
Santerica L Benoit
Carmen K Bernard
Alexis N Berry
Phil Berry
Helen D Beverly
Gladys C Bih
Joanne L Bilotta
Shantasia Bing
Janet Binyanya
Ruth A Biza
John D Black
Patrice Blackman
Simona S Blackshear-Robinson
Malik A Blair
LaTonya Y Blake
Markech S Blake
Gregory J Blanchard
La-Tanya D Blanton
Keith Blue
Sona Bokosa
Barbara Bolcavage
Kelly Bolcavage
Tiesha Boles
Carline Bolivar
Angela P Bonavico
Demia L Bond
Daryl G Bonner
Jennifer G Boubel
Dianne T Bowdary
Maurice A Bowie
Felecia D Bowles
Retha Y Bowman
Shellie M Bowman
Vicky M Boyd
Virginia J Boykin
Eric M Boykins
Nicholle N Brace
Syvella Brantley
Terreanna J Braud
Kadeem N Brewer-Nunn
Torry J Brewington
Turquoise D Brittingham
Kaylyn P Brock
Troy A Brock
Sakeena E Brooks
Sonja L Brooks
Queen M Broussard
Misty Brown Pearson
Akina J Brown
Arita Y Brown
Dawn M Brown
Derek K Brown
Desiree S Brown
India Brown
Jennifer Brown
Ronetta L Brown
Rosemary L Brown
Sterling Brown
Tanaisha A Brown
Tarkeisha Brown
Tony L Brown
Yesenia V Brown
Natasha L Bruton
Sylvia Bryant
Ricky L Bugg
Gilroy A Buller
Cetera J Bunche
Thomas A Burch
Bessie Burley
Gwendolyn R Burnes
Jevertus D Burnett
Joyce D Burnette
Cinnamon B Burton
Jazmine M Burton
Connie J Butler
Jakaiah E Butler
Joanne C Butler
Sandra O Butler
Ervin Byrd
Ferman D Cabiness
Edison Cabrera
LaToya M Cadlett
Petetra L Caldwell
Asim S Calloway
Chris J Cannon
Petrina L Cannon
Sandra J Cannon
Amy Carey-Wollaston
Theresa A Carpenter
Marcus D Carradine
Debra Carrington
Briana N Carter
Marialyce L Carter
Rodrick E Carter
Tarnesha M Carter
Camara J Cash
Ebony M Cass
Terry J Caston Headen Black
Miriam Castro
Simon Chacha
Nicholas Chavez
Monica M Chavis
Lessie L Chester
Markus A Chew
Jamaine Chisholm
Natashia A Christie

Douglas A Chu Eze
Hyun-Mo Chung
Andrew J Chupp
Dawn R Churchill
Ebony N Clark
Mia M Clark
Susan A Clark
Cynthia M Clarke
George Clarke
Nataisha A Clay
Chad J Clayton
William W Clayton
Faryal D Clouden
Vincent T Coates
Evelyn R Coker
Raven D Cole
Walter M Cole
Colette Coleman
Rodney E Coleman
Grant S Collier
Jessee T Collier
David D Collins
Shelia Collins
Sheri P Colvin-Jackson
Derry Conley
Ken Constant
Shelvy L Convert
Rita I Cooma
Donald H Cooper
Lana E Cooper
Regina F Cooper
Benjamin F Copeland
Cheryl D Copeland
Sandra R Copes
William Counts
Montrella S Cowan
Yarnell M Crawford
Rhonda R Creek
Ajahni M Crenshaw
Merle D CrimDuBois
Jesselle R Cromartie
Kortnee M Cross
Candace R Cuello
Jeremiah C Cummings
Laron L Curtis
Adriene S Daise
George Dandridge
Stacie L Daniel
JanLe Daniels-Johnson
Anika Daniels
Tysheen B Daniels
kwame A Danquah
Wanda Darden
Antonio T Davis
Cynthia M Davis
Daniel Davis
Heather J Davis
LaVaisha Davis
Rashaun L Davis
Ricky D Davis
Tiara N Davis
Vanessia Davis
Angela M Dawkins
Kimberly A Dawkins
Martial A Ddamba
Kawunde
Myra Dean
Roslin E Dean
Tesalia L Deavers
Anara Dennen
Rodney L Dennis
Tonya Dennis
Terrell Denson
Naomi Derrick
Monica K DeVaughn
Thomasena Deveaux
Khady Diaw
Ruth Diaz
Tamara A Dickerson
Shamia Diggs-Long
Hope O Dike
Onyinyechi B Dike
Damon P Dillard
Mikadya S Diltz
Danielle L Dion
Alexandra Dittmer
Alisha T Dixon
Futina Dixon
Estelle Docilet
Trina Dominguez
Eliton Domond
Kevin J Donaldson
Kimani E Donaldson
Joseph V Donkor
Stephen M Dorrell
Tanesha R Abass
Robert F Abercrombie
Anne W Kimani
Ashanique T Kimble
Hottensiah N Kimori
Deneen D
Douglas
James P Doyle
Genelle M Drayton
Anissa M Drummer
Jimmy L Duggans
Jentle L Dukes
Brandie J Dula
Cheryl L Dunaway
Shelly B Dunaway
Delon Duncan
Gina S Duncan
James Duncan
Rodney L Dunn
Aurelia V Dyson-House
Kevin Edmondson
Whitney M Edmondson
Alfred Edwards
Andrea I Edwards
Donald A Edwards
Keyon N Edwards
Stephanie T Edwards
Prosper E Ehunyi
Ime P Ekanem
Jude T Ekeh
Victor O Ekenavie

Thomas C Elder
Jeffrey Elhoffer
Justine R Elliott
Shayquana Elliott
Altina K Ellis
Paul C Emenogu
Etheldreda I Enongene
Christina N Epps
Ese S Eruvwetaghware
Rosi R Espinal Diaz
Chase Evangelista
Debra A Evans
Kimberly Y Evans
Alice A Eyong
Douglas A Eze
Leviticus D Farmer
Alethe Fatherley
Gregory Faulcon
Crystal Feathers
William L Feggins
Robin L Feindt
Jessica Feliciano
Sisse S Ferguson-Torok
Terri L Ferrell
Sohail J Fiazi
Liliana E Fidalgo
Marvetta D Fields
Tyion A Fields
Carla E Finley
Adetunji Fisayo
Joy O Fisher-Afolabi
Gary C Flemmings
Carmen H Fletcher
Grace Fletcher
Janice Florence
Abel Flores
Pauline Flowers
Shavona L Floyd
Awie G Fofana
Emmanuel F Fomukong
Solomon M Fon
Ernestine M Foncham

Willie S Forbes
Tyrell L Ford
Charese B Foreman
Dija Forte
Epiphany B Foster
Kelly A Foster
Bertrand P Fote
Eva L Foushee
Jannell Fox
Domonique A Franklin
Nsidibe Fred
Diane Fredercik
Tamika R Frederickson
Erika L Freeman
Misty N Freeman
Anthonia N Fregene
Jason S Fuessel
Joel Fuessel
David E Fulcher
Tiffany C Fuller
Yolonda Fultz
Kianna R Funderburk
Pamgrace Gachenge
Althea Gaines
Jade D Gaines
Hector J Galvan
Victor C Garcia
Dennis R Garland
Lynn M Garrett
Monique S Garrett
Milvia Garrido
Shunta Garvin
Bridgette R Gasaway
Kevin Gatewood
Veronicah Gathoni
Fabian O Gayle
Sequoia T Gaylord
Michael J Gee
Zambia Geiger
Cuthbert M George
David Germain
Ericka M Gibson

Janice L Gibson
Rose W Gichomo
Gila S Gilamichael
Donna W Gilchrist
Sharlene C Gillespie
Armstead Gilliam
Tanya L Gillie
Gregory P Ginyard
Virginia Gitau
Alice W Githii
Airionne R Givens
Anthony Gladney
Aisha K Glenn
Marcus R Gloster
Shelley Gloster
Jalauna C Glover
Dorothy S Godia
Nadia A Goldsmith
Connie J Gomez
Peaches E Goodwill
George V Gordon
Katherine M Graciano
Christian Graham
Jessica E Granillo
Donte C Grant
Joseph K Grant
Wendy R Gravely
Sherod Graves
Kyla M Gravitt
Eric D Gray
Essence S Gray
Marco A Gray
Yukema Y Gray
Lynette D Green
Tabitha Green
Angela M Greene
Cynthia G Greene
Valdrada S Grissom
Robin L Gross
Felicia M Guerrero
Kyana N Guidry
Yvette R Guizie

Krystal M Gumbs
Rey Z Guzman
Tisha M Hagues
Wintana Hailemariam
Lauren Hairston
Lusine Hakhverdyan
Darin O Haley
Alton L Hall
Joseph W Hallisy
Cassandra L Hammond
Laura Hammond
Erin D Hanks
Robbie D Hansley
Debra K Hanson
Harold W Hardee
Darron D Hardmon
Pamela E Hardnett-Armistead
Deborah C Hardnett
Valencia H Hargrove
Dianne E Hargust
Erika Harp
Jacqueline Harris
Janell A Harris
Malcolm Harris
MJ Harris
Nichole A Harris
Stacy L Harrison
Delann Harshman
Kemisha N Harvey
Vanessa P Hatfield
Cornelius L Hathorn
Guadalupe Y Hau
Anthony Hawkins
Charlene D Hawkins
Christina I Hawkins
Anita L Hayes
Cassandra Hayes
Michael T Hayes
Terrance L Hayes
Yvondra C Hayes
Koran J Haystings
Kendrick R Hayward
Burnell E Haywood
Glen F Healy
David S Hearn
John J Heck
Marti L Heinz
Hyacinth Henderson
Robert Henderson
Chameka M Hendricks
Julia A Henson
Mitzi J Hernandez
Keith D Herring
Jabari J Higgins
Susan D Hightower
Brenda Hill-Johnson
Myosha S Hill
Sidney E Hill
Rhoda M Hines
Pamela E Hoggard
Donald Holder
Kymbrea M Holder
Alexis A Holifield
Richard Holley
Crystal Hollingsworth
Barbara R Hollis
Aravia L Holloman
Elijah E Holloway
Vanessa Holloway
Rosario B Holmes-Onyekwere
Troy D Holt
Michael D Hooker
Althea J Hooks-Young
Perrion Hopkinson
Lisa Horsley
Shelia L Houston
Andre Hubbard
Brandy Hubbard
Randy Hughes
Shakeema Hughes
Angela P Hulett
Jerod Hunt
Hale D Hunter
LaSheena C Hunter
Tiffany Hurdle
Kia B Hurst
Pamela T Idahosa
Ndidi C Ihim
Tolawo R Ilesanmi
Ziva B Israel
Domminique Ivey
Onuaku P Iwugo
Clydell Jackson
Eric S Jackson
Janet E Jackson
Jeanine D Jackson
Larry D Jackson
Latoya N Jackson
Lovonia L Jackson
Margaret D Jackson
Monique E Jackson
Norma G Jackson
Tontalia L Jackson
Trinita H Jackson
Yaminah S Jackson
Darryl Jacobs
Donna Jarrett-Mays
RaShanna G Jasmine
Margarette Jeffers
Marcus E Jeffries
Margel D Jenkins-Palmer
Ava Jenkins
Demetric Z Jenkins
Jake F Jenkins
Keenan J Jennings
Sharon L Jennings
Melissa A Jeter
Amajuoritse S Joey
Desmond I Johnnie
Xavier S Johnson-Reeves
Beverly M Johnson
Brian L Johnson
Crystal S Johnson

Faith W Johnson
Geoffrey T Johnson
Ivory Johnson
Jaquan T Johnson
Kimberly Johnson
Lynette L Johnson
Marriel M Johnson
Roderick L Johnson
Rodolfo Johnson
Rose D Johnson
Roy L Johnson
Steven L Johnson
Bockarie Jombor
Marilyn L Jones-Barnes
Alphonso D Jones
Alton Jones
Antwane F Jones
Brenda V Jones
Eula L Jones
Hardeep N Jones
Jenese L Jones
Paula L Jones
Shirley A Jones
Tamia Y Jones
Tangela T Jones
Tara L Jones
Tavaris K Jones
Thomas H Jones
Mahoghany Jordan
Javarah Joseph
Tuesday Y Joseph
James G Joynes
Loise W Kabui
Nancy W Kabuki
Meduwodzi K
Kalin-Samlan
Sheku Kallon
Kevette M Kane
Kenyange Kaounde
Mark Kaplan
Milca A Kaplan
James M Karangu

Liz Karanja
Sudha V Kargi
Aaron Kariuki
Catherine W Kariuki
George Kariuki
Hiram G Kariuki
Jacinta Karungi
Doron Katriel
Dimitra T Kaulu
Deogratias M Kawunde
Patricia Kearney
Leuel Kebede
Crystal E Keckler
Keith T Keemer
Karen Keith
Lorna A Kelley
Oscillious Kemp
Adrianne L Kendell
Pauline W Kiarie
Samuel Kibe
Edward M Kiiru Joi M
King
Wilma D King
Ruth N Kinyua
Ruth M Kioko
Cristine F Kitzinger
Ronald Kleiman
Reina A Kluender
Samuel E Knight
Lola B Knights
Maria D Knott
Seyi Komolafe
Ernetta C Lagarde
Charles J Lambus
Joshua L Lang
Brandy L Langley
Melvin L Latimer
June Laudat
Leslie L Lavert-Green
Dunstan O Lawanson
Janet M Lawrence
Kevin R Laws

Crystal N Lax
Emani D Lee
Joanne B Lee
Sharon C Lee
Sonique Y Lee
Charles E Lemons
Lakeia Lemons
Michelle E Lennard
Tameka S Lenoir
Jeraldine Leonard
Melissa M Lester
Brian E Lewis
David Lewis
Keisha A Lewis
Kila J Lewis
Patricia R Lewis
Sonia T Lewis
Frances K Li
Jhenileen A Libongco
Carolyn M Lightle
Kimora Link
Markehan D Littles
Brian Litz
Annie L Livingston
Lamar E Logan
Marilyn Logan
Chasidy A London
Michelle Long
Adrianna Lovett
David N Luksic
Tanya Y Lyles
Inga R Lynch
Natasha Lynch
Natasha Mack
Linda D Macklin
Reggie Maclin
Patricia C Maduakor
Mark D Maguire
Angelique V Mahan
Faith N Maina
Shane A Makell
Kepha O Makori

Aidiah S Mallory
Frenesi Anne Mangonon
Jacqueline L Mansker
Anita M Manuel
Antonio S Marcus
Lori G Martin
Lori L Martin
Jose A Martinez
Immaculate W Masamba
Evelyn J Maschat
Roderick O Massey
Terri Matlock
Shalun Matthews
Maria Maymi
Curtis M McBurnie
Ebony M McClatchey
Blessin D McCoy
Tomika L McCullough
Shante McFarlane
Marcus L McGee
Samantha S McGee
Bonnie McGlothin
Caryn J McKee
Ectasi K McKenzie-Rollison
Jasmine V McKenzie
Tanya M Mckinley
Janelle Y Mckoy
Edgar L McLean
Elijah McMillian
Kimberly R McMorris
Gerald L Mcnair
Erika L McNeal
Michael T McNeal
Mahasin A McNeely
LaQuana T McNeil
Kezon McNeill
Marcia L McPherson
Edric M McSween
Larry D Meade
Issac R Meador
Joseph N Mecha
Doris Meintzschel
Daniel Mensah
Vincent Mensah
Shaynie S Mercer
Angela R Merriweather
Toussaint L Miller-Bey
Aries Miller
Bennie L Miller
David T Miller
Derrell Z Miller
Mary B Miller
Kevin G Mills
Chonita L Milner-Vaughn
Shawn J Milton
Anita R Minor-Clifford
Erika S Minor
Kia L Minor
Renee D Minus
Francisco E Miraval
Eugene Mitchell
Keva L Mitchell
Marvin L Mitchell
Shalonda L Mitchell
Caroline Mkubwa
Rose K Mogire
Rosa H Molina
Sharon S Montague
Angeles M Montaner
Helena E Montgomery
La'Quashia N Moody
Montarius O Moon
Terry L Moore Sr
Donna M Moore-Jackson
Carlette D Moore
Jeff L Moore
Melvin Moore
Sharon H Moore
Tana J Morehead
Angela Y Morgan
Akia J Morris
Carina M Morris
Monica M Morris
Antonio Mosby
Vinara Mosby
Callen M Mose
Francis M Mose
Keisa L Moss
Wilfred N Motaro
Darnell K Mote
Darrell M Mote
Teri T Moten
Will M Moten
David Muchendu
Tabitha Muchiri
Ameenah S Muhammad
Munirah L Mullen
Yufressia Mumba
Keith A Mumphery
Ruth W Munene
Jideraph W Murigi
Dallon T Murray
Rami Mustafa
Josephine K Musyoki
Joan Mutesi
Gladys N Mwangi
Jacquiline K Mwangi
Maria Cynthia W Mwangi
Sarah N Mwangi
Simon N Mwangi
Patrice R Myers
Bethany L Myles
Zuri K N'Namdi
Ferrus W Najemba
Elizabeth M Nalyanya
Rose T Nantongo
Georgene F Nathan
Pape Jean Ndiaye
Daniel N Ndogo
Ere Ndukwe

Lydiah W Ndungu
Jessica Nelson
Roxana Nelson
Raymond O Nembhard
Stephanie Nevels
DeMario D Nevins
Terry D New
Nancy M Newkirk
Tamia M Newman
Tiajuana Newton
Christine W Ngaara
Dorcas W Nganga
Collette Ngewih
Stephen Ngo
Jenny N Ngugi
Daniel W Ngunjiri
An Nguyen
Loan B Nguyen
Siphiwe Nhliziyo
Jewellyn A Nickson
Johnell Nickson
Dinorah Nino
Nicholas M Njeru
Emanuel O Njoku
Elysee M Njontu
Esther M Njuguna
Mercy T Nkesi
Grace A Nkosu
Melanie Norman-Jones
Tony Norwood
Virginia Nsiegbu
Benson A Nsunwara
Emmanuel B Ntim
Satcher An Kham Nu
La Verne C Nunfio
Risper M
Nyabeta-Motanya
Newton M Nyairo
Sospeter M Nyakeraka
George M Nyakundi
Michael A Nyakundi
Lyna M Nyamwaya

Doreen N Nyangau
Esther M Nyariki
Alfred A Nyarko
Yamikani C Nyenga
Mary O'Dell
Kelvin O'Kelley
Folashade Obadunke
Pamela Obare
Damaras L Obi
Jane Obutu
Benjamin B Obwoni
Joyce E Odoom
Opeyemi A Ojelabi
Nancy O Okeyo Ssali
Nnamdi-Raphael Okoye
Olufemi S Olatunji
Ashley C Oldham
Charles Olimi
Charles A Olimi
Christopher Oliver
Nathaniel D Oliver
Shawn C Oliver
Shontese N Oliver
Akinnuga A Olusanya
Sharon C Omire
Gladys K Ondari
Cynthia A Oneal
Jonathan Oneil
Tshanna Oneil
Udodiri J Onwubiko
Amber-Rose M
Onyekwere
Arial B Onyekwere
Elvis L Onyekwere
Erron Onyekwere
Covenant
Onyemenaonu
Joan P Onzia
Awura A Opoku-Reeves
Milton N Oriku
Alice U Orji
Pamela M Ortiz

Ola Osanyinjobi
Valencia L Osby
Akinola J Oshodi
Doreen K Otachi
Breana C Ozenne
Robert P Paige
Joann M Pantoja
Santiago
Ilona D Parker
Patricia L Parker
Prince Z Parker
Curtis Parks
Tranyce A Parmer
Valerie
Parris-Richardson
Felicia Parrish
Johnathan R Patrick
Taneah B Patterson
Timothy D Patterson
Gwendolyn Patton
Sophia L Payne
Frederick N Peal
Lakitha Pearl
Pamela G Percival
Lynneia Perkins
Jacob M Pernell
Kirstie R Perry
Nisha D Persaud
Cheryl A Peterson
Priscilla H Pettaway
Russell E Pfeifer
Deanna L
Phillips-Porter
Briana L Phillips
Keniti U Pinkett
Dimeta J Pittman
Monica R Poe
Oswald E Poindexter
Clairees O Poitier
Gerald Policastro
Gerald Policastro
Gerald Policastro

Charese Pollard
Nadege C Ponkin
Lawrence Poole
Samonne L Porter
Tara Porter
Jabari Postell
Carol A Powell
Jarrard A Powell
Michael Powell
Anthony C Prater
Kennisha C
Pressley-Smith
Felicia D Price
Debra J Prince-Durand
Sherri Pruitt
Brandon C Pryor
Jeanna L Pryor
Jeremy A Pryor
Nehemiah Pryor
Raven Purvis
Jeannette E Ramcharan
Jacqueline M Randall
Lauren Randall
Ayvonne V Reese
Stephanie D Reese
Michael A Reeves
Tamara L Reid
Skylar D Rembert
Dwayne C Rhames
Carolyn E Rhodes
Ada L Rice
Karen R Rich
Anne M Richard
Catherine M King
James I King
Charles E Richard
Chereace A Richards
Stanley G Richards
Allen D Richardson
Carrlynn A Richardson
Lajeune T Richardson
Elliot J Ricks

Kinji R Ridley
Walford D Riels
Edward T Riley
Reginald Riley
Kim Rimmasch
Juan A Rivera
Shamika P Rivers
Kimberly N Roberson
Sunday J Robert-Eze
Morgan Robinson II
Charissa C
Robinson-Garrett
Calandra A Robinson
Charles W Robinson
Jonte Robinson
Louree S Robinson
Sarah A Robinson
Paula J Rodgers
Robert L Rodgers
Janie R Rodrigues
Josephine Rodriguez
SheNice K Rodriguez
Valerie M Rodriguez
Sheree N Rogan
Karen B Rogers
Kevin J Rollins
Diana Roman
Cinnamon J Rosa
Megan L Rosario
Joyce E Ross
Richard J Rossi
Harold Rowson
Bernorris L Rozier
Dana N Rucker
Courtney T Ruffin
Catherine W Rugano
Katresia A Rush
Leroy E Russ
Karen E Russell
Alice K Rutere
Latina Sabb
Lakysha Sager

Didier Anton Saint-Cyr
Arell S Samuel
Ruby S Samuels
Arlene Sanchez-Vinas
Earlene Sanders
Thredda C Sanders
Olatokunbo Sanusi
Mark G Saunders
Courtney R Scott
Elizabeth Y Scott
Michael Scott
Shawn R Scott
Vanessa M Scott
Judy A Scriber
Ebony Scudder
Tamonie Scudder
Grace M Sebo
Karen K Sebro
Stacy S Segal
Venus J Senior
Abaddon E Shaitan
Ceara S Shaw
Tangie A Shepherd
Elea L Sherrod
Deborah Shields
Deborah L Short
Deondra Short
Lisa Sibert
Richard F Sielicki
Kennedy N Sikini
Ruth K Sila
Andrea J Silas
Deedra Simmons
Nichelle J Simmons
Connie Sims-Smith
Tracy L Sims
Bryan Singletary
Marcus J Singleton
Brandon A Slater
Catherine Y Small
Genevieve Y Small
Joshua E Smalley

Louis T Smalls
Jacques Smit
Joyce A Smith-DeLancy
Paula P Smith-James
Dellwyn K Smith
Karen Smith
Lawrence Smith
Mavo Smith
Misti D Smith
Roy Smith
Shanelle M Smith
Sophia L Smith
Tonia L Smith
Tony R Smith
Yolanda Smith
Brenaye L Snell
Lauren R Snell
Shelley M Sohne
Helen M Somanji
Patricia Soria
William R Spady
Brittaney Spann
Kabrina T Spates
Claude T Spence
Deyka C Spencer
Anita M Squire
Rekisha Squires
Robert S Ssekandi
Thomas W Stancil
Thomas W Stancil
Charmel N Stanley
Gwen G Staples
Karen M Starr Johnson
Tracy R Staton
Tara J Stevens
Alan A Stewart
Christina D Stewart
J Nelson Stewart
Sharon L Stewart
Shawnda L Stewart
Inez B Stringer
Deondria R Sullivan

Benjamin Surprin
Brandon Swanston
Sequan M Swint
Larry Swinton
Sonia S Sykes
Imelda Tabares
Margaret Tabiri
Donna A Tabor
Craig Talley
Cassandra A Tangong
Michael D Taplin
Frank J Tarimo
Concela Tarver
Hassan R Tate
Nicole A Tate
Katrina Tatem
Camile Taylor
Jyoti R Taylor
Tanya D Taylor
William E Taylor
Lucy N Tengeri
Portia M Thiam
Allison M Thomas
Barry V Thomas
David H Thomas
Enomowoyi I Thomas
Fayona R Thomas
Isaiah Thomas
Jordan S Thomas
Mitchell O Thomas
Nicole Y Thomas
Shalanda M Thomas
Tia Thomas
Vita D Thomas
Billie C Thompson
Danielle Thornton
Quentin D Thornton
Rashida K Thurmond
Deniecia J Tillman
Tonee A Timmons
Justin X Tinglin
Shirnice D Tinnel

Judith M Todd-Ginyard
Adebayo O Togun
Willie C Tolbert
Amanda S Tomlinson
Kevanta L Tompkins
Edward F Toole
Lisa Toomer
Michelle H Toomer
Edgar L Torres
Hai N Tran
Travis L Treece
Iris Trice
Natalie R Trotman
Cicely D Trotter
Mwadi M Tshoba
Ashante L Tucker
Tessie T Tucker
Kwabena O Tuffour
LaShona R Turner
Gregory D Twilley
Brandon G Tye
Charnise N Tyler
Dianne E Tyler
Sandra P Tyler
Vivienne C Udoji
Luis E Valdez Jauregui
Descarte O Valnor
Deirdre S Van Walters
Edwin R Vargas
Elisa Varnedoe
Alvin A Vassor
Tyrone A Vaughn
Ruben O Vazquez
Natika V Vess-Sheffield
Monica Villareal
Daniella Volkovitz
Tracey L Waddell
Francina
Wade-McQueen
Lisa S Wagstaff
Daniel N Wainaina
Micah Wainwright

Dana P Walden
Dominique M Walker
Karen A Walker
Shane R Walker
Vinis C Walker
Gilda Wallace
Robin A Walls-Couch
Kevin M Walls
Joseph T Wanene
Esther A Wanga
Caroline Wanjiru
Tosha R Ward
Sharhonda A Warner
Jimal M Warren
Alice W Waruingi
Angernett N Washington
Anthony W Washington
Carl Washington
Donielle M Washington
Eugene R Washington
Kelli M Washington
Kimberly C Washington
Stephanie R Washington
CJ Waters
Kiva V Waters
Christopher M Watkins
Rufus Watkins
Shir-Rhea M Watson-Moore
Kerry D Watson
Kristopher D Watson
Miles H Watson
Tomeka S Watson
Jalisia M Watts
Henry S Waweru
Curtis L Weaver
Denise T Webb
Timothy Webb
David W Weeks
Elizabeth A Weeks
Charissee Weidenbosch
Regina Welch
Joseph M Wells
Kesha M Wells
Teel S Wesley
Dale A West
Melissa D West
Sharonda M Wheeler
Bennie White
Claudette White
Derick White
Gladston E White
Mia T White
Roderick G White
Shamia White
Shonta D White
Theresa White
Sheri N Whitfield
LaToya T Whitsett
Vicki Wicker
Jilonda L Wilcox
Nicholas S Wilkins
Isabelle Williams-Brown
Qiana N Williams-Ford
Aliyah C Williams
Aris L Williams
Beverly J Williams
Bianca L Williams
Cornell L williams
Davine M Williams
Denise Williams
Dominique N Williams
Gary D Williams
Joseph L Williams
Keshay J Williams
Kim Williams
Lamondes D Williams
LaShawn Williams
Lucillious D Williams
Mandy L Williams
Maria B Williams
RahSaan C Williams
Tracy Williams
Wallace J Williams
Yolanda R Williams
Brandie V Williamson
Karen M Willis
Maximo R Wilmore
JaNeshia C Wilson
Jermaine L Wilson
Monica S Wilson
Takisha Wilson
Udonia D Wilson
Adrienne A Winbush
Charla Y Winbush
Charles Winfrey
Tamika Wise
Taneeka C Witherspoon
Deon R Wood
Talethia L Woodard
Leticia D Woodland
Valerie L Wrice
Brentley R Wright
Chauntelle Y Wright
David M Wright
LaTonya Wynne
Nygaa Yemariamfere
Hellen N Yiapan
Jade E York
Alexis M Young
Cynthia C Young
Diane M Young
Michael A Young
Naqunia Young
Monique N Younger
Olushola B Yusuf
William T Zeigler
Maurice R Zereoue
Mawugnon D Zouhongbe

Made in United States
Orlando, FL
04 November 2026

90207836R00056